Turning Toward Morning

by

Joe Cardillo

Northwoods Press

ISBN 0-89002-235-4

Books by Joe Cardillo
A Legacy Of Desire
Delicate Passions And Madnesses
Living Outside The Law-Tales Of Love And Rage

Northwoods Press
Thomaston, Maine 04861

Acknowledgements:
Many of the poems in this collection first appeared in ***The Crab Creek Review, Footwork, Nuclear Cafe, The Sierra Madre Review, Third Eye,*** and ***The Yellow Butterfly.***

Cover Photo by Darlene S. Cardillo

Contents

Part One

Part Two

This book is dedicated to my two beautiful sisters, in appreciation for all of the roads we have traveled together.

Part One

I come, embrace you,
fall completely into your fire. . .

We have exhausted trillions of winters and summers. There are trillions ahead, and trillions ahead of them. . .

Walt Whitman

Prospects For Art And Peace In The Hands Of Pure Yang

Listen:
A child weeps black music.
A *child* weeps black music.

*

The house on Apple
Wood Road is filled
with good things,
isn't it?
The smell of wood,
real wood.
Of cushions someone's
perfumed face dipped
into. Of fathers
and their children
pressed in glass,
reflecting in the glass
of other faces.

*

In the dark outside
one wolf hunts
another. Loves her
on a bed of stone.
Across the palest
face of winter's
moon. Two perfect
points driving
deeper into the
darkness,
becoming the darkness.
Their wails blowing
through the night
like the music of

black flutes rising
and falling in the wind.
Rinsing away the scars
of too many days,
of too much light, final
like a soft lid
dropping over half
the human world.

*

Child, I too want
more darkness.
Black music.
The weight of stone.
The smell of wet
earth and fire.
The taste of smoke
and fish in the
darkest braid of
yin. Where shadows
slip between our
fingers, fill up
the space of empty
hands. And bodies
still in the cellar
of consciousness
fit perfectly together.

*

Inside the night
howls burn
in the heat of
plastic bulbs.
A woman who is
half man clicks on
lights all over
the house.

A man who is pure
man pulls on the
television,
blasts the darkness
from the room.
A child, not yet
man or woman, yells.

*

Outside a single tail
splits the moon in two.
Like a perfect arm
raised in its own
emptiness.
Sprays of white breath
disintegrate vaguely
across the sky.
Communicating everything.

A child, still unafraid
of the dark, hugs a tree.
Looking for comfort in the
hardness of old bones.
Feeling for his heart
pounding in the kindness
of wood. He hides.
From the sound of
rifles snapping
in the dark.
A neighborhood of
men and their half
women crunching
over fallen leaves.
And mostly from the
blaze of metal,
from pure yang,
ripping up everything
it does not understand.

He turns away,
howling black music
no one else can
comprehend.
One last song to
his brothers and sisters
who will die
with their eyes cursed
forever open,
with their whiskers still
wet, shining in the
mechanical light of men,
with their ears raised
high, as if forever
listening.

Adam, he cries, do not
forget the blood of
Cain. Do not forget the
womb of my mother.

Return Flight

The distance between
the point that is our
beginning and that
which is our end does
not diminish.
But I am sure of one
thing. We have
forgotten it exists.

*

Tonight I imagined
a bee orbiting the
moon. On a full
moon night.
Stinging at her lips.
While the Snake casts
its skin, pirouetting
all of her edges.

*

In New York, my home,
it is the time to
pick apples. To fill
baskets with berries
and tomatoes.
To taste air brushed
with cider and the
fire of leaves.
For men and women to
cuddle like mice,
using each other's flesh
to hide from the cold.

*

Vastness will make
life small again.
There will be no
automatic weapons
carried into streets,
men clicking rifles
outside temple walls.
Holding knives like
bread loaves or
something sacred.
There will be no
broken bodies, bleeding
to the incredible sting
of human breath.

*

The sky will fill
with the pale light
of many suns.
Pull up perfect wheat
and corn.
The moon will form a
perfect zero among
imperfect stars.
Cities will hum their
hallowed song, smoke
in the heat of sewers.
Children will learn how
to hustle everything,
including Christ.
Here where *making it*
is worth the soul.
Men and women will
pretend not to count
their hours, all
huddled up in the hands
of time. As long as
the sun rises. As long

as the moon spits zeros
across the sky.
Pushing herself rimlessly
over silos and fields.
Like a fallen angel
ready to do anything to
conceal their astonishing
hardness.

(The bee bites at
the moon.
The Snake casts
its skin.
The moon swallows
its head.)

*

On this, my deepest flight
into the equation that
separates beginning from
end, I return sure of only
one other thing.
The door that was mine
will not open to me anymore.

Athens

*

In Greece there is much light.
The white light of morning.
The iron light of day.
And the neon light of Marlboro,
Adidas, and Champion. Champion.

*

In white air. Beneath
the windless haze there
is the slow *almost silent*
cry of breaking. A
pouring out of stones,
giants sucked pale under
the sun. Their voices
floating like spirit
through the hollow heat.
Bleached and burnt.
This is pure ruin.
Filling up wherever there
is space.

*

Beyond the Plaka. Beyond
all of the markets. Where
hardly anyone notices
the smell of fresh breads
and corn souring in midair,
in fumes spit out of squealing
cars and angry mopeds. A
blindman sells toy maracas in
the shade, begging anything.
His woman. Already dressed in
black kneels on crusty knees.
Her fingers, fat worms scraping
through crumbled cobblestone
for one flung coin, one. As
his face droops over old bones
frozen at the clearest peak
of nightmare.

Delphi

There you are. Tongueless.
Without women now. Standing
as if I were meant to touch
where hardly any man ever does.

In Delphi, in the presence
of giants and gods.
Someone has hacked off hands
and even arms. Has mended
thick masculine fingers
permanently to weapons aimed
forever at nothing.
Like your iron-tight testicles
poking through the Twentieth Century.
Shattering in the grip of laser
logic like hollow shells.

You want me to know all that
was your breaking. To watch it
rupture this bone-dry air like
swollen veins emptying their
entire past in one mad gush.

Outside a young boy, maybe 16,
clutches his radio to his lap.
Smiles as it mouths English
he vaguely understands
sloppily across his legs.

I want to walk away from you.
From all the pain that was
your ruining.

In America it is easy, how we
talk of peace. And of accepting
all of the bad inside the good.
As if that were just a part of

growing up. Or learning
to live with
history repeating itself.

On the radio, a woman sings. Something
about filling up her life.

I am empty now. Small and without
such great resolve. Letting your cold
consciousness wrap around me like slow
wind. Freezing me to its very center.

Hedy

All day long she
worked outside.
With men. The only
woman.
In sweaty shadows.
Beneath butchered
pigs slung on hooks.
Behind her bloodstained
table. Piling meat and
fish by the handful.
Feeling for the
suffering inside
all the slaughter.

Once she asked if things
were the same in America,
all over the world.

At night we watched
neons spit their noisy
light across the street,
Acropolis brightening
in the distance.
A Reenactment of its
burning.

Hedy lay still in
her dim hotel light.

Her home for 14 years
now. You could see
plaster swelling on
overheated walls.
104 degrees most days.
Bugs that bit crawling
on buckled floors.

Her hair shined like
damp coal in moonlight.
Spilled over skin the
color of oak.

I reached for her.
Opened her to the touch
of fingers, the urgency
of lips.
"No," she said, "I was
not meant to love. Can't
you see? It is too late
now." she said.
"Too late for what?" I asked.
"Too late for anything," she
said, but slaughter."

Looking Out

Husky moped whines
curve along chewed up
streets. Scorch the city's
spine, storeys high.

> *This is what I see*
> *for 14 years now,*
> *Hedy once said.*
> *Hard to breathe sometimes.*
> *You will see, she said.*
> *You will see.*

In the shade of an old
eaten awning. A boy
with arms thick as legs
wrings a rooster's neck.
Slips a knife below its
skin and cuts.
His dogs kick up broken
glass and gravel, complain.
A woman, his grandmother,
curses in Greek. The dogs
obey her, the dogs do.

Winos don't piss on walls
here. They don't have to,
so many empty buildings.
But reactionaries are
different. Smear paint
wherever there is space.
KKE streaks, the color of
blood. Brushed on doors,
on walls and bridges.
Communism whispered in Greek.
The sound of a covenant
everyone pretends not to hear.
But everyone does.

This is not America,
Hedy once said, though
the only other American
she'd ever known taught
her to arch her back
until she ached. To
whip her hair back-n-forth.
Left her rock on tape and
a few turquoise rings.
That is not America either,
I said.

At the end of the street
is a park. Filled with
flowers, thousands.
The smell of figs, peaches,
grapes, fresh dough and
warm oil.
The cathedral is there.
Its dark hump frozen still
against the gold Athens sky.

Two kinds of people go
to the park, Hedy said.
Those to take pictures
and those to make prayer.

And which are you? I asked.

I cannot afford the camera,
she said. *I cannot even*
afford the time.

Away From The Mainland

There was no dancing
on this part of the
island. Not many
tourists. Or cars.
Mostly donkeys and mopeds.
Two or three jeeps.
The beach was nothing.
Filled up twice a day
with small boats biting
at the coast like fish,
emptying supplies. Meats
and poultry packed in
plastic sacks young women
slung over dirty donkeys.
Colas they'd roll up in
their skirts and carry
like babies.

*

At night fires snapped
at the shore.
Tents were pitched.
The smell of cooked fish
and warmed breads swelled
up everywhere.
About a 1/4 of a mile
away were Germans. A family
of men clumping with the
men, always combing the
coast together.
While their women, all of
them the color of milk,
squatted before the fire.
Where there was always the
sound of sucking, always.

*

Hedy ran to the edge
of the sea, her eyes
glistening like wet caves,
her lips, a thin pink moon
smiling. She cupped her
hands. Filled them with
water she let spill over
her stomach and legs
and for a long time just
watched me from the center
of her silence as the Aegean
licked at the moon sliding
up the sky behind her.

The sea is absolute
feeling, she once wrote,
rubbing even stone precious,
smooth again. Trembling
as each fish enters her
deepest parts, lives and
dies at her very core.

*

I was full of America.
White logic. TV peace.

*

She wrote about Theo.
A journal full of
how everything
could have been.
Till she found him.
Opened up like the men
slit pigs,
fast and noiselessly.

*

The coast was warm beneath
us. Our fire strong.
Hedy's hair smelled of
earth and wind as it smeared
across my face, her mouth
deep and trembling as the sea.

I rubbed sun-bleached lips
across her back.
Felt our knees disappearing
deep into the sand as our
heads filled with the music
of waves and the rhythm
of the sea.

*

In the fall there are few
fires along the coast.
Hardly any tourists.
Only the natives, walking
among the chickens and goats
and cats. Carrying a meal
in their palms.
And sometimes there is rain.
A lot of clean hard rain,
sweeping up everything
the world has discarded.

Courage

You say the
symbol
must be marked
in blood or land,
the cross, maybe,
X'd onto the souls
of men and women
who dare hold
their eyes to a
light that will
not diminish
until it has stripped
their faces to the
bone. Or radiated
their hearts to a
dead stop.

I say it is invisible.
Like the breath of
a woman passing
through the lips of
a man.

What you want is
a fast blackout.
Like the worm that
kisses the throat
of the cactus and
dies to save the
life of a stone.

We Eat Together

We eat together
every night,
passing cups
that carry the
warmth of hands,
the smell of
different countries.

You talk of F-15's
burning up the sky
at treetop,
of rifles your fingers
will steam on,

while the terrace
fills with the
sound of children
I imagine already
dead.
Pieces of voices
whipped around
the world
like the carrion
of a million
deja vu I could
gather in my hands
and spread across
your lips,
push inside your
nostrils and ears
until you stop
pretending
how different
we all are,
until you can taste
the sound
of your own voice.

What It Is Like

There is no beginning, no end.
There is no exit.
There is only now!

*

It is almost night.
The skyline reddens
deeply as bruises.
The room stinks
of smoke and sweat.
He is hungry, thinking
about how easily skin
opens to the spray of
bullets, bone splits.
Just the other day
three men gunned down
26 pedestrians. 26.
Markota arrives.
Her hair is dark
and wet, smells always
of the land.
Her face bleeds.
She will not even think
of leaving this place,
her father missing.
Her sister and mother
murdered one year.
She weeps. Screams to
everyone in French.
Sometimes I wish I were dead,
she says, and then I think
maybe I have already died
again and again and again.

They hold each other, not like
lovers but like outlaws

of some sacred writ.
          He touches his mouth
          to where she is bleeding.
They fall, like this, to the
floor. They are hungry.
Will do anything to lessen
the pain. Anything.

Maybe Tonight

Light drains from
the sky over Old City,
buries its head in
the soft horizon
as iron angels pour
one last song howling
down the face of
the moon.
Tired voices settle
on the white breath
of donkeys,
glide in and out
of stone hallways
where men will pray,
holding their rifles
like candles,
their prayer books
like ice.

Cats die in roads
here. Unnoticed
as pigeons and
old people do in
America.

Women wrap up in
veils, sit on
warm sidewalks,
bushel baskets
between their knees.
While sons sell
what's left
of morning's bread.
And it still surprises
me how many stomachs
can hurt
so late at night.

*

Michael calls me in
for tea. Tells me
again about his wife
and children.
Their fourth is on
its way.
Maybe tonight.
Maybe tomorrow, he says.

He cannot go to pray
with the others
And he does not want
to go to America either,
he says. Because this
is where he was born,
and this is where he
must die.

He has painted me
another cup,
all morning long
it took him.
I will bring it home.
Keep it filled with
teas and milk and
coffee the color
of his eyes.
But I will not pray
for him. Not once.
Because he would
not want me to.

*

In the road outside,
a camel rises.
He is not as wild

as those that mull
in fields before
the dessert roads,
and, I think,
he knows it.
Night, to him, is
a chance to act as
if no one else is
around. To change
his lot. It is the
only time he can
act this way.

*

Tonight I walk home
alone, watching the
stars sing their
silent credo.
Knowing that anything
louder will be
too much.

Ghost Town

The mist over
this town
whitens like
a shroud
not even the sun
can lift.
It is dead.
It will stay dead.
Its only survivor
in tongueless,
half his mouth
buried below an
eucalyptus tree,
in a bunker
not far from here.
There are no ghosts,
not really.
Only the sounds
of one man
praying
with his hands.

Talking Of Lebanon

. . .took 500 trucks
two months to
clean out the mess
of arms.
Illegal, all of them.
Terrorists no one
could imagine.
And all the shooting.
Cousin against cousin.
It never matters who.
How you'd laugh,
but it wasn't really
funny. 537 were
already counted dead
and maybe more.
How everyone has guns
and is afraid.
So people climb their
roofs at night,
and you can hear
them shaking,
saying something about
revenge, you say
people like us
can never understand.
But that a man could
shoot his daughter,
murder his wife
and go on living.
So people don't go
near the streets
at night because of
what could happen.
And how it doesn't
really bother you,
except for in the
morning.
When someone else is
always dead.

Sometime Late At Night

A bird nearly
freezes
to my window,
his wings broken
like small hands,
his face
shaking against
this plane of
night.
I yell something
about damning
and sleep.
But he stays
anyway,
bowing his head
just a little
as if to say
he is sorry
but that this is
his covenant.
That pain this
real
cannot darken
in the middle
of the night
the way
televisions do
on our
bookshelves.

Turning Toward Morning

Part One

Darkness floods
the room
thick as mud painted
on our eyes,
and the sea sends
her long wet melody
sighing
through our ears.

*

We lie separately
tonight.
But I can hear you
turning,
your breasts and legs
cuffing into a
mattress you cannot
stand, arms jamming
under a pillow your
nostrils draw the smells
of 3,000 years from,
body oils of Arabs
and Christians and Jews,
sweetening your brain
like the dreams of
an unborn child rolling
in your belly
or an angel kissing
you where no man
ever could.
Your lips fatten,
so much sleep pulling
the blood from
your cheeks down.

(It is good, the taste
of blood sometimes.)
Your legs bone into
a braid, warm below
blankets you hate (the
smell of someone else's
lust and ashes, you say.)
And your fingers reach
into the ebony of dreams
as if wrenching one last
melody, bluer than all
of the rest.
Bluer than anything
that has ever burned in
the pit of your brain.

*

Our song begins:
Israel, oh Israel, oh Israel. . .

The moon swells over
the sea,
completely on fire.
And a thousand springlets
of water surface
like pools of tears
streaming from tunnels
deeper than anyone
could ever believe,
gushing and gushing
through the dark
like the wails of
martyrs
dying in the arms of
no one,
singing the song of
Hejira.

*

Part Two

It is morning.
When our stomachs
usually ache the most.
When we share hard
breads to fill them,
pray in different
tongues.
When we must let
our bodies say
all our mouths have
forgotten.

In '59 it was easy.
We used to take a
stick of glass.
Wash it clean as a
cross and slash
our wrists in ragged
spirals,
mixing bloods
that made us
brothers.

*

And so I pray. . .

Your face turns
itself to
almost black,
and you are thinning
like an animal
that needs to be fed.
Your hair, dark waves,
washes down upon

your forehead,
across your white-shawled
back, your eyes
sucking me into their
Semitic caves,
your lips
kissing the milk
from my mouth,
from my fingers.
And your skin roughens,
probably all of the
sand and wind,
as I enter you,
chasing you down the
allies of yourself,
ancient stones
that smell of fruit
and sweat,
of old shirts and pants
piled for trade,
of chickens and fishes
and urine.
So you run among the
goats and cats,
squinting your coal-black
eyes to see if
I am really following you.
But I want to stop you.
Love you and love you
into trusting
that I don't need to
examine you
under 1,000 tons of cobalt
to know all that the years
have done.
I can feel pain even in
the darkest of places,
with hands paler than the
bottoms of your

nomadic feet. I can.
And I want to scream
screw the colas
and all of the phony
silver and gold
in this whole city
and just hold you until
our love murders us
in the sugar-scent
of almonds,
and we can sprawl out
in the mind of God
and watch the sky
spill itself into
tomorrow.

But you run undauntedly,
the sun ripping up
the haze above you as
you race toward tents
sagging their skin
like ravens nailed to
hot dry earth.

Women wearing coats
to their ankles
pull scarves around
their faces
like sinproof forcefields
as you pass,
babies slung in their arms
like old sweaters,
bellies already filled
with another
almost year of duty.

Suddenly you turn,
your arms aflame,
your mouth and eyes

and hair, all ablaze.
A vulture arrows
through the wind,
crashes hard
into the ground
before you.
And I come,
embrace you,
fall completely into
your fire,
both of us weeping
the voices of children,
the blood of Abraham,
Jesus and Mohammed
until our bodies
explode,
and the energy
of centuries surges
through our arms
and necks
and heads,
until it cuts
its way to
our hearts
and burns us into a
consciousness
brighter than any sun.

The vulture is dead.
The dessert
has blossomed
into an oasis of
fruit trees
and grasses,
pools and pools
of water
sucked up from
wells
deeper than the

tombs of Atlantis.
And we are alone
and naked
and unashamed.

*

Now that our bread
is broken,
our prayers said.
You can take this
American wrist
of mine, cut it
and squeeze it to
your own parted flesh,
forgetting everything
that you have ever
felt but the
stinking pain that is
about to join us.

Once you said that
we must always
be welcome
in each other's
house.

What I am trying to
tell you is that
we must forget
about our separate
houses
and live
inside each other's
blood.

Part Two

Times we trusted driven in deep. . .

Wildcats

. . .For Mignonne and
Rusee, the two cats
whose actions and
souls and love have
been the subject of
ALL my CAT POEMS since
the summer of 1982 -
when I first saw
Rusee finishing the
remnants of a rabbit
she had killed.
Anyhow, these cats
ARE real. Everything
I have ever said
they do is real.
Everything. And they
have taught me more
about poetry than any
book or human tongue
ever could. . .

*

Rusee

The grass is all
mudded with blood.
What's left of a
dead rabbit,
maybe, hardening
up to the touch
of flies as the sun
disappears
behind the pines.

*

It is always in
the morning or at
dusk you hunt like
this, the taste of
blood wailing in
your mouth and you
willfully entering
the space where
dark and light
spin apart
breaking reason
like an ancient bone
your nostrils
will flare to.

*

Christ Almighty,
I have seen you
claw a sneaker to
shreds, shit in
the flower gardens
Jackie spent all
day painting.
(Though when I
finally saw the
canvases, I almost
laughed, thinking how
the turd may have
been more meritorious.)

*

The house is full
of company the exact
color of American
Cheese, with stories
about who's sticking
it where in these

inflationary times and
how *high cholesterol*
kills.

*

I imagine a creature
that is half man
half beast
springing from the
grass, fingers
searching a sticky
heap, yanking up a
strand of gut and
swallowing it,
his face all eaten
with radiation,
his eyes already
wincing the pain of
malignancies
in the city's saline
wind. To him, I look
like the ghost of his
own assassination.
I unfold this flap
of dusk like the
last flash of heat in
the face of suicides.
Where there is no
flower left to slow
the blade that hacks
the world in two.
Where fair-haired angels
sway like Jezebel
waiting to pluck out
the eyes
of father and son
at the altar of their
holiest communion

together.
And where lips,
tightened as the
mouths of rats,
kiss us awake and
leave us to fear the
sound of ourselves
finding ourselves.

*

I enter.
You are stretched out
on a limb, tail hanging
like a rope.
You know why I have
come. And still you
lie there like an old man
asleep on his couch.
Suddenly you burst
into the hollow that is
our silence,
run to where the moon
will soon be rising,
leaving only the certainty
that we have come upon
this place together,
that we have made our peace.
And I return to where
the sky is almost night,
bringing with me
the smell of cat and wood
and good earth.

Nikki

*

'67, '68 scribbled on
the backs of photographs.
Long years. Times we
trusted driven in deep.
So slow they could never
wash away. Not with age.
Or tears. Or anything.

(Sometimes, even now, when
I think of the three of us,
I know healing could only
mean more death.)

*

Randy (1948-1968)

Holding Nikki from behind.
Small breasts only she
hated, buried beneath
his calf-sized arms.
(Nikki, I can still feel
how you pulled my face
to yours, your mouth
open wide. Soundless.
All of the pain scooped
out. Bled away transparently.)

Two years. So much
waiting, Nikki would say.
For the touch of lips
she had opened everything to.
The smell of work wrung
into pants she had
pressed her face to.

Eyes that had made hers go
wide. Silent.
At eighteen. To already
know of waiting like this,
she said. For lies only
old women could endure.
Like aging. Something
that far away.
Like Vietnam (always
raging in her head.)

But it was not the bullets
that killed him.

It was heroin.

*

The Moon

The two of us walking.
A day when the sky was
ice. Wood smoke twisting
through chunks of fat clouds.
So much snow. And Nikki's
hand shoved all the way
down to the bottom of my
pocket, clenching mine.
It was morning.
But we could still see
the moon. Floating in
between clouds. Thin circles
of light pressed against
the sky.

She told me of having
two fathers. A mother
drunk on beer from
morning always calling

her a whore. And all
the hate. Her mother's.
Her own.

*

The Cottage

It was rented.
Not much of anything.
Bare floors. Oil light.
Smelled of old furniture
and hot cast-iron.

I can still remember
the shock of so much heat
on cold faces. Of snow
melting instantly.
Of slippery collars
and socks. Frozen shirt
sleeves. The tug of
buttons so hard to squeeze
through wet slots.
And Nikki's fingers,
trembling through all of
the space between us.
Long arms reaching under
my shirt, around my back.
Friendship dissolving
in the quick blur of
eternity pressed into
an instant.
Without promises.
Without secrets.
A place we would
never go again.
But it was everything.
It was
exactly what we wanted.

*

Nikki

Someone said she has
two children now.
Teaches in a college
not far from here.

Where Are We Going?

Remember when our
world was suddenly
water?
How we swam
our mouths together,
tied them everywhere.
Before we tried
to crawl, our bellies
never really meant
to scrape the earth.
Before our eyes grew
lids to help us turn
our backs against
the sea, our bodies
never really knew
what it was like to
shake inside the wind.
But how, after all,
it was the wind that
carried the smell
of Judas, even then.
The first sighs of
meat and blood
forever forced into
shapes they could
never understand,
but someday pretend
themselves into forgiving.

Annie, when I love you,
I can still taste
the salt beneath your
arms, inside your milk,
between your hairs.

Annie, last night
I dreamed a creature
still swimming miles
in the dark.
And he was laughing.

This Is How I Come To You

The bridge is empty
as I cross,
sways with the grief
of old wood.
Down the road,
your face is a blur.
Your body cries
like ink spilling
through red dusk.
Even the cows have
left, fearing the
grip of bad weather.
But you, you call
to me anyway.
And I come, imagining
myself headless,
breaking into the
very center of your
terror.
And you embrace
me anyway. As if
the only thing that
matters is that I
am there.

Faith

I loved
watching you
nurse
the squirrel
and
pour the shepherd
water you
might have had
yourself.
It was as though
a man
could learn
to square himself
off with
almost anyone
and with the
earth,
could want to
give back
a little more
than the rest
of the world
was always
taking.

Your Face Is Turning

Your face is turning
liquid, ice below
the thunder slap
of steel.

(Some say you
are responsible
for your own face.
The caricature
below the skin.)

There is an emptiness
about you.
A pouring in and in
and in like waves
at midnight
crashing over the
bones of amphibians,
sucking up the sand
or floating like
fingers through the
thin hip of the moon.

(Some say it is
possible to be
born again
after so many
years of dying.)

It is startling
the way you *almost* enter
into dark places.
The way your body
could almost abandon
you like a spoon of fog
in a light that would
be your dying.

In the woods a
wildcat licks the
blood birth from
her fur.
Her nostrils flaring
midnight air,
her whiskers jabbing
into the night,
eyes reflecting the
dark slope
of sky between her
knees. Tail, damp
and glistening
as the first plucked
rib, as the first loop
of soul spun inside
a creature not yet man,
not yet beast.

But you, you have
learned to embrace
only the sun.
To suck the poison
heat of
enlightenment
stiffened in your
veins like broken glass
clotting its way to
your heart.
Exploding you where
no one can hear.
No one
ever hears you anyway.

But the creature who
could enter you more
swiftly than sin.

The creature who is
almost you is still
listening.

And In The End

The moon burns white,
washing the world
clean of itself.
A cougar swallows the
dust from another's
pads, bites at the
fur below her tail.
And a cool wind
sweeps the earth
like the breath of
an unknown planet.

A man and woman
lie together on
the very edge
of the world,
glistening in the
wet light of so
much moon.
She has painted
her lips with the
blood of berries,
her nipples with
the honey of bees,
filled her mouth
with the sweet sweat
of flowers and grass,
the blue sugar
of stone.

He leans long into
the wind, sucking
the sea from its
veins, rewinding
the earth through
all of his spaces
like the genetic

code for *bird* and
moose and *bear*
bursting through
his corpuscles like
the spit of God
streaming through
an empty universe.

He runs, maybe a
mile or so.
Gathers armfuls of
vines and pink roses.
Brings them to her.
Twines them through
her hair
as they lean gently
into the night,
entering the dark rush
of every wind
of every sea,
the deep tunnel-taste
of each other
learning to make
sound break
into the clearest
of light.

The Author-

Joe Cardillo lives in Albany, New York. He is currently teaching English and Creative Writing in a college in northeastern New York State. He has previously published two chapbooks of poetry and one full length book, ***A Legacy Of Desire.*** *His work has earned him several awards and he has been published in numerous books and literary magazines. He is on the editorial board of* ***Esprit - A Magazine For The Humanities*** *and is the coordinator of several writing projects.*